Oh, My Credit!!

Building Solid Personal and Business Credit

By: Cornelius Edrington

Copyright © December 2021

All right reserved. No part of this book may be reproduced in any form, or by any means without prior consent of the author and publisher as a collective, except brief quotes used in reviews.

ISBN- 9798419846531

Contact US:

Spect Publishing LLC
PO Box 929
West Chester, OH 45071

**We Helped This Author Self-Publish
And We Can Also Help You Too**
Contact -Crystell Publications
PO BOX 8044 / Edmond – OK 73083
www.crystellpublications.com
(405) 414-3991

Printed in the USA

ACKNOWLEDGEMENTS

First and foremost, I would like to thank Diamond, I couldn't have done it without you. Everything you have done has been eye-opening to me and I want you to know that I notice every detail. We inspire each other to new heights. Next, I want to thank my children, y'all make me want to be better. I want to thank my mom, brothers for believing in me. I want to thank Neil McNeil, you banged it out on the keys. Right on, Bro. I want to thank John Bell AKA Boogaloo, we spent a lot of time in the editing room, our cell. Finally, I want to thank God for giving me the strength to make this dream come true. Anyone I forgot, my bad, I love you too.

CONTENTS

CHAPTER ONE
The beginning of my credit life……………….........................1

CHAPTER TWO
How credit works and why it's important……………….5
How FICO credit score is calculated………………………..

CHAPTER THREE
Dispute letters…………………………………………….16

CHAPTER FOUR
Credit inquiries……………………………………….35

CHAPTER FIVE
Building credit: Different trade lines needed……………..39

CHAPTER SIX
Secured and unsecured bank loans…………………….....42

CHAPTER SEVEN
Secured and unsecured credit cards ………………….48

CHAPTER EIGHT
Retail credit card/lines of credit…………………………..55

CHAPTER NINE
Authorized users, cosigners, and trade lines…………….59

CHAPTER TEN
Credit card perks and potential pitfalls…………………….64

CHAPTER ELEVEN
Other interesting credit facts to know…………………..77

CHAPTER TWELVE
What it's going to take to fix wealth gap……………….85

CHAPTER THIRTEEN
Conclusion, Author's personal story and encouragement… 89

Cornelius Edrington

CHAPTER ONE
The beginning of my credit life

While I was incarcerated, I wanted to start building up my credit. The first thing I did was have someone in my support system on the outside sign me up with a Credit Karma account, which let me know that my credit was shit, low 500s. Credit Karma let me know that there were several things on my credit that I needed to dispute. Things like a $300 Capital One credit card bill, $1000 cable bill and a $500 electric bill. Normal things we tend to neglect.

NOTE: On Credit Karma you can only check 2 of the credit reporting agencies; Equifax and TransUnion. To check your Experian score you will have to get a separate account.

Not knowing about credit, I didn't really understand that I could dispute these things or work out a deal with the creditors to get these delinquent accounts handled. I never even knew that I should try.

I ordered a book called *The Credit Secrets* and it became the credit bible for me on my road to getting my credit in good standing. The first thing I did was learn about what a "Dispute Letter" is, how to write them, and how to properly send them.

To start, I got the $300 Capital One credit card bill

successfully disputed and removed from my credit report on my very first try. Once it was removed, I saw that this one move instantly increased my credit score. Mentally, just seeing what this did for my credit, I became hooked on everything that had to do with building my credit and also helping other people build theirs.

Pumped up over my success with the Capital One dispute, I started the process of disputing the $500 electric bill. This was not as easy as the credit card bill dispute. As a matter of fact, they gave me pure hell about disputing it. From this dispute I learned that although you have to take all of the steps equally to fight things on your report, you will not win all of these fights. For instance, the electric company adamantly refused to do ANY wheeling and dealing on that $500 bill. There was no negotiating with them. They wanted the full $500, which I eventually paid after I understood that they were not going to budge on it. Once again, another stain was removed from my credit report, and my credit score instantly was increased. Although I had to pay this delinquent electric bill, it was well worth it because my ultimate goal was to increase my score. So, even when doing disputes, you will win some and not have to pay anything to get the old debt off your report, but there will certainly be others that will have to be paid. Regardless, getting negative things off your credit report for the purpose of building your credit is the whole point of this, so even if you have to pay some of the accounts off, you will be rewarded with a much higher credit score.

Now, I was getting somewhere.

The process was not without unpredictable bumps in the road. After seeing negative things come off of my credit report because of hard work, came the bumps. Once I started getting things straightened out with negative accounts on my credit, others seemed to pop up. That's where the $1000 cable bill came in. Because I was diligent in what I wanted, when I gave them resistance they backed off, and the mark was removed from my credit report.

Another win.

Now my credit was up to 620.

At this point I was beginning to understand the effect of having multiple accounts, being in good standing in those accounts because of consistent on time payments, and having the accounts over a certain amount of time to establish positive payment history.

I paid off three cars. That had a great effect on my credit score. I paid off three 90 day same as cash credit lines from Value City Furniture that were valued at over $3,000. These lines now showed up on my credit report as Paid as Agreed.

Now I was feeling really good about having a steady increase in my credit because of the work I was doing to make that happen. From seeing the results of my work, I started talking to other people about credit. I learned other things I could do to further increase my credit score. Things like becoming an authorized user on somebody's account who has good credit. This is also known as piggybacking, something I will explain in more detail later.

Somebody in my support system made me an authorized user on their credit card and that immediately boosted my credit score beyond anything I could've imagined at that time.

746 Equifax.

Mid 700s in both Transunion and Experian.

I applied for my own Visa credit card. They gave me a $500 credit limit. I used the card consistently and paid the bill on time every month. This reflected on my score in a positive way.

Then, another bump in the road came by being careless with who I trusted with items that effected my credit. I let somebody have a car that was in my name, that I had been paying the note on every month. He was supposed to maintain the payments on the car. Unbeknownst to me, he was late on 2 payments. That was a huge hit against me. It took almost 100 points off of my credit score. A score I was busting my ass to build. I learned, and I'm sharing with you, that protecting every aspect of your credit is an absolute must because the same way positive things have a great impact on your score, negative things have a devastating impact.

Because of this experience with the car, I was also stuck with those late payments showing up on my credit report. I can't overstate how important it is for you to understand that late payments show up on your credit report for SEVEN YEARS!!! But don't worry because for every on time payment you make on your accounts, you will maintain good standing and the negative effects of the late payment will be diminished with time.

Through the awesome ups and the downs I knew I would overcome, I trusted the process and never got discouraged. My goal was building my credit and that's exactly what I did. I started building my credit in 2019 and now I have over $16,000 in available credit

You have to trust the process.

CHAPTER TWO
How credit works and why credit is important.

The purpose of credit is allowing you to acquire access to funds or assets without using all of your own money to accomplish it. If you are trying to buy a $50,000 home and you don't have that amount of money laying around, you can get a mortgage for that house and make monthly payments that might not amount to $500 per month. For this credit, your creditor will charge you a regular monthly payment that is only a fraction of the amount of credit you are receiving.

The payment you make for this credit will include an interest rate, which will be low or high depending on your credit score. To be brief but to the point, you pay more for credit when your credit score is bad, than you pay when your credit score is good. This is why we all should go to great lengths to protect our credit score and the financial credibility that comes with it.

Your credit score is calculated using a formula that is centered around 5 financial factors that are unique to you.

The 5 Finacial Factors
&
How They Make Up Your Score

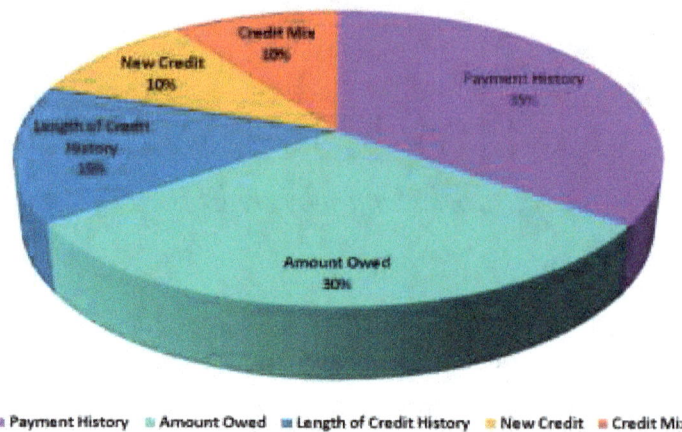

1. Payment history. This accounts for 35% of your total credit score.
2. Amount owed. This accounts for 30% of your total credit score.
3. Length of credit history. This accounts for 15% of your total credit score.
4. New credit. This accounts for 10% of your total credit score.
5. Credit mix. This accounts for 10% of your total credit score.

The Fico-8 standard says the lowest score is 300. The highest score is 850. Your credit is classified in 4 different categories. Poor. Fair. Good. Excellent.

300 - 559 is considered poor credit.
560 - 669 is considered fair credit.
670 - 799 is considered good credit.
800 - 850 is considered excellent credit.

Credit Scores Factors

Factor	Percentage
Payment history	35%
Amounts owed	30%
Length of credit history	15%
New credit	10%
Types of credit used	10%

Range: 300 - 850 (Very Bad, Bad, Good, Excellent)

Not knowing or understanding how credit works in general is a huge mistake that literally millions of people make. By looking at your credit report, creditors can see everything they need to determine if you are worth the risk of having funds lent to you, and at what interest rate they should take on that risk. Also, a good or bad credit score is reflected in things like down payments on practically anything from buying cellphone service and cars, to buying a home. A person with a good score can buy a new cellphone service without any down payment at all, while a person with bad credit may have to pay $1000 as a security deposit for that exact same cellphone service. A person with good credit can buy a car with no money down, while a person with bad credit may have to pay a steep down payment for the same car. A person with good credit may have to pay as low as 5% down on a home, while a person with bad credit may have to pay upwards of 20% down. This reality is true within any sector you can think of where goods and services are being given to somebody in exchange for a promise to pay.

The payment history in your credit report demonstrates your track record of paying your bills on time, or not. It shows the amount of "paid as agreed" accounts," paid off accounts, past due accounts, collections accounts, etc. To avoid being seen as too risky, it is in your best interest to keep your payment history positive because it is the biggest thing used to determine your overall credit score.

PAYMENT HISTORY

You've made **98%** of payments on time

	J	F	M	A	M	J	J	A	S	O	N	D
20...	✓	✓	✓	✓	✓	✓	✓	✓	✓			
20...	✓	✓	✓	✓	✓	✓	✓	✓	✓	✓	✓	✓
20...	✓	✓	✓	✓	✓	✓	✓	✓	✗	✓	✓	
20...				•	✓	✓	✓	✓	✓	✓	✓	✓

✓ Current   ✗ Not current   • No data

The amount of debt you have tells a lot about your credit movement and how savvy and responsible you are. Also considered here is the ratio between outstanding debt and total amount of available credit you have. Being close to maxing out your available credit will reflect negatively on your credit report. To manage this, your best bet is to only use a certain percentage of your available credit, this way you show consistent usage, which reflects awesomely on your report, while at the same time still having the bulk of your credit available to you. Only max your credit out when you have built a history of making consistent payments and you are naturally close to reaching your max anyway. Creditors love this so much that they will approve you for credit lines faster when they see that you have the positive "debt to income ratio" that comes from doing what I just named here in this paragraph.

Credit Health

Credit Factors

Payment history **99%**	HIGH IMPACT
Credit card use **4%**	HIGH IMPACT
Derogatory marks **0**	HIGH IMPACT
Credit age **2 yrs, 9 mos**	MEDIUM IMPACT
Total accounts **12**	LOW IMPACT
Hard inquiries **5**	LOW IMPACT

The length of your credit accounts in your report are really important in determining your creditworthiness. The longer you have an account open that you are paying on time every month, the better it looks on your report. The less time an account is open, even if you pay it all off, the less impressive it looks on your report. Basically, even if you have the money to pay an account off that you've had less than 3 months, don't pay the account completely off. Make a couple more payments on the account before you go ahead and pay it in full. This shows the perfect transition from establishing the credit line, to using it, to paying the bill on time every month, to paying the whole account off.

NOTE: Example if you have a credit card for 6 years and you add 2 more credit accounts, it will look on your report as if you've had the 2 new cards for 2 years apiece, because your 3 accounts will be divided by 3. This will lower your credit score a little bit because it will look like you just grabbed up 3 credit cards in a short period of time. To combat this dilemma, start early building your credit and be sure to keep certain credit lines open. To use a real life situation of this going badly, just today (July 9, 2021) I saw on the news that millions of Wells Fargo customers are pissed off because Wells Fargo is suddenly closing all of their personal credit lines. Just imagine how somebody who has had this account for years, even decades, must feel. These customers are about to have a hit on their credit report, a closed account, that they had no say or control over.

A mix of credit accounts shows your ability to maneuver around different types of credit lines in a responsible way. You don't want to have a large number of just one type of credit line. Instead, you want to mix it up and move in and out of different kinds of lines to have a paper trail of how you handle yourself financially.

New credit lines are also important in your credit score and are directly in your control. New credit lines are what happens when you seek and receive new accounts. The first step in the process of new accounts is a credit inquiry. You fill out an application to get new credit and the creditor runs an inquiry on your credit report to determine if they should give you an account. This is good when you get approved for the account. But when you don't get the account it is bad because inquiries on your credit report effects your credit score. If you have a whole lot of inquiries into your credit, especially within a 12 month timeframe, your credit can take a hit for it. So, be strategic about the amount of new credit lines you seek and when you seek them.

A credit score of 300 — 559 is frankly terrible, A score this low comes from completely neglecting your financial responsibilities, not paying bills on time, getting a whole lot of useless inquiries into your credit report, going a long time without any credit at all which gives you no credit history, letting credit accounts become so far neglected that they end up in collections. This tells creditors you are a high risk person to consider for credit. The consequence of having your credit slip to this level is being forced to pay extremely high interest rates on the very few credit accounts you may be lucky enough to get approved for, huge down payments on items you want to get on credit, having to pay high premiums on things like insurance accounts, and being subject to victimization from predatory lenders who will take advantage of your poor credit score to price gouge you on loans.

But, don't be discouraged.

Even with a terrible credit score, you can follow the steps laid out in this book, and others, to build your credit to the highest level. All you have to do is have the patience and willingness TO follow the process. Doing the exact opposite of what you did to get on this credit level will get you on a higher level.

A credit score of 560 - 669 is better than the above level, but still far from where you want to be at, the highest level. This second level means that you either started at the above level and have done some things right to slightly improve your score, or you barely have any credit at all. When you are on this level you have to challenge negative marks on your credit report where practical and pay off any accounts that can't be challenged.

If you are on this level because you don't have any credit history, you should get small lines of credit where you can with businesses that offer them and report payments to all credit agencies.

NOTE: I will list a few of these types of businesses in the reference section in the back of this book. You will be familiar with nearly all of them.

Having a credit score of 670 — 799 is good. This is the level you work your way up to by being consistent with paying all of your bills and credit accounts on time. You also get to this level by elevating within your credit lines and still staying consistent with your payments. For example, you have a credit card with $1,000 and you use it regularly and pay every month on time. When you are nearly at the end of the limit you may likely be offered a higher credit limit on that line. Once you take on the higher limit and continue to pay on time you will not only be demonstrating the ability to take on more credit and manage it, but you will also be extending the payment history on that account, which reflects greatly on your credit report. Making timely payments and eventually paying off several of your accounts in full will also get you to this level. Once you are on this level it means your creditworthiness is recognized by lenders and your ability to get to the next level will not be difficult.

The credit score of 800 — 850 is your ultimate goal in building your credit. Once you have this level you have a lot of responsibility to maintain it because of the consequences of slipping up. You get to this level by using the previous level to build up limits on some of your credit lines to maximize the showing of payment history consistency and also length of history on those lines, by paying off multiple lines in full, by getting new credit lines and maintaining your timely payments, by minimizing the amount of senseless inquiries into your credit report. Even if you are filthy rich, staying on this level takes work! Don't make the mistake of thinking that you can slip up on this level just because you have a lot of money and then fix the slip up by throwing money at it. That's not how credit works. When you screw something up, there is an amount of time that you have to deal with the consequences of seeing it on your credit report and all you can do in that event is avoid that mistake in the future and regain your reputation for consistency by watching your credit report closely and knowing every single detail about what you have there and how to utilize every detail to your benefit. Remember, the credit bureaus do not use discretion, discrimination, or favoritism to determine what a person's credit score is, or who will be hit with negative marks because of mistakes made, late payments, too many inquiries in a short period of time, or defaulted accounts. They use a system that doesn't consider anything outside of the numbers! If you are ill, it doesn't matter to the scoring system. If you are incapacitated, it doesn't matter. A late payment will show up negatively and that will affect your credit score in a bad way for years!

Having and building credit is important for us because numbers don't lie. The wealth gap between Black people and White people in America is astounding. When you take a look at some of the corresponding data in practically ALL financial areas, you will notice that the gap is equally disproportionate. According to the Urban Institute, which is a nonprofit research organization, a 2019 study found that 50% of White people have a FICO score of at least 700 points. This same study found that only 21% of Black people have a score that high.

ONLY 21%!!

They found that 18% of White people don't even have enough credit history to create a score at all. They also found that 32% of Black people are on that same level of having no credit score at all.

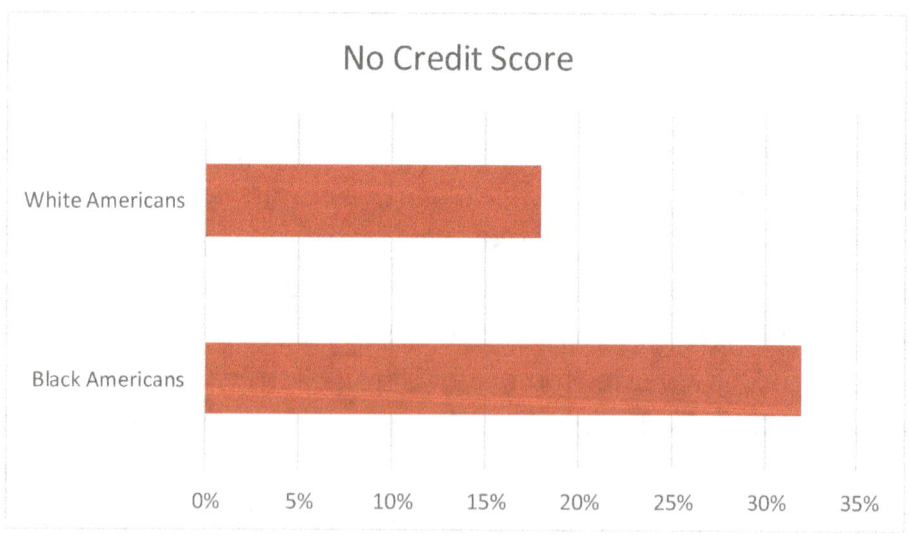

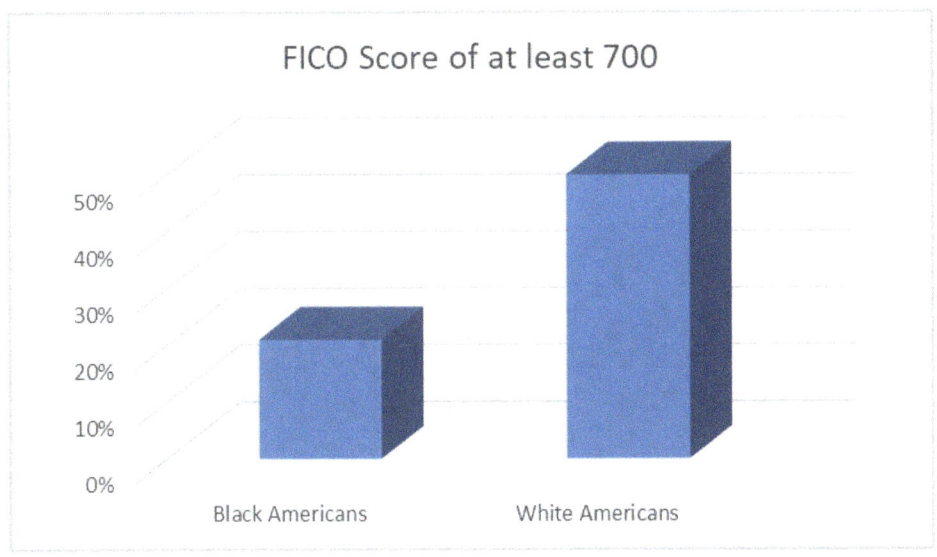

There is no coincidence that when I started building my credit my overall financial situation went to a new level. I now find myself able to have things and pay them off creating even more credibility on my name, even more creditworthiness. The benefit of having good credit is that it gives you the ability not just to go out and pay for consumer products that keep you looking good or driving good, or pay off bills that keep you feeling secure that your family has a roof over your heads, or receive the lowest of insurance policy premiums, but good credit also gives you the freedom of using it to GET AHEAD. This means it allows you to maintain managing your family's finances in a responsible way that gives you the freedom and space to jump out there with a business idea that would never have been possible with your 9 to 5 job alone coupled with bad credit or no credit.

CHAPTER THREE
Dispute letters and how to use in building credit

Not all of the harmful information on your credit report is going to be correct. This could harm your score if you don't do what you need to do in order to have the incorrect information fixed or removed. If you have accounts on your credit report showing debt that you don't actually have, you have just two options: Pay it off just to get the bad mark off your credit report, or dispute the bad mark with the holder of the account claiming you owe them money. The former would be a last resort, as nobody should be paying off a debt that is wrong unless there is no other remedy available because you have exhausted every other option. The latter is done using a series of what is called "Dispute Letters".

A dispute letter is a valuable tool for you to use when you look at your credit report and see some accounts or debts that are inaccurate. Dispute letters should be clear, concise and straight to the point. This
letter should not have a lot your emotions or opinions in it, only the facts of what the problem is and any accurate and relevant legal references like citations of a law or judicial case law. The shorter the letter is, the better.

Oh, My Credit!!

NOTE: Three stages of real dispute letters will be in the following part of this chapter along with dialogue and examples describing when you should use them.

Let's say for instance you had a cell phone service that you switched from in favor of a better service elsewhere. The previous company hounded you for the remainder of the money you owed on your account. You didn't think you owed the money so you refused to pay it. Then, considering your credit, you made up your mind to send a payment to the previous company just to be done with them. The problem is, when you decided to make that payment, the company had already sold your debt to a collections agency without you knowing it. So, when you paid them the money, they kept it and sent it to the collections agency who bought the debt. Now, when you look at your credit report, guess what you will see? A strange company showing up as an account you don't recognize with a dollar amount owed that looks familiar. When you contact that company to see who they are and how you owe them money, they let you know they're a collections agency who bought your defaulted account from the cell phone service provider you owed money to. When you tell them you never did business with them and that you paid the previous cell phone provider the money that they are claiming you owe and is now showing up on your credit report, they shut you down. They have already paid money for the account and they want you, or whoever, to pay for it. But, you have disputes at your disposal to challenge accounts like this and have them completely removed from your credit report.

While speaking on the phone to managers in the collections company as high up as you can get, you should also send off dispute letters to the company to make them remove the account from your credit report. This kind of debt does not belong on your credit report for two reasons.

1. You don't owe the money anymore to the company you originally did business with after you paid the balance off.
2. You never had any business dealings with that collection agency, and in order to owe them money they will have to show otherwise, which they cannot.

This is the first letter that you will send to the collections company, or any other company with a negative mark on your credit score that you want to dispute.

NOTE: Each of the dispute letters must be mailed out using certified mail to ensure that your letter has to be signed by a representative of the company upon its delivery. This way no company can deny receiving it.

Letter #1.

    Date
    Your name
    Your address
    Name of company on your credit report
    Address of company on your credit report
    Re: Account # (as shown from company on your credit report)

To whom it may concern:

Oh, My Credit!!

This letter regarding account #_____, which you claim that I owe $_____. This is a formal notice that your claim is disputed.

I am requesting validation, made pursuant to the Fair Debt Collection Practices Act and the Fair Credit Reporting Act, along with the corresponding local state laws. Please note that I am requesting "validation", that is competent evidence bearing my signature showing that I have (or ever had) some contractual obligation to pay you.

Please also be aware that any negative mark on my credit reports (including Experian, TransUnion, and Equifax) from your company or any company that you may represent, for a debt that I don't owe, is a violation of the FCRA & FDCPA; therefore if you cannot validate the debt by showing my signature on a contract placing me in business with you to pay the balance I'm disputing, you must request that all credit reporting agencies delete the entry.

Pending my timely response to any evidence that you submit, you are instructed to take no action that could be detrimental to any of my credit reports.

Failure to respond within 30 days of receipt of this certified letter may result in small claims legal action against your company at my local venue. I would be seeking a minimum of $_____ in damages per violation for:

Defamation
Negligent Enablement of Identity Fraud
Violation of the Fair Debt Collection Practices Act (including but not limited to Section 807-8)
Violation of the Fair Credit Reporting Act (including but not limited to Section 623-b)
Please Note: This is a reasonable attempt to correct your

records, and any information received from you will be collected as evidence in the event that further action is necessary. This is a request for information only, and is not a statement, election, or waiver of status.

Please be aware that dependent upon your response, I may be detailing any potential issues with your company via an online public press release, including documentation of any potential small claims action. I am also including a copy of my complaint to the organizations below:

CC: Consumer Financial Protection Bureau
CC: Attorney General's Office
CC: Better Business Bureau

My contact information is as follows:

Your name (printed NOT signed)
Your address
Your last 4 of SSN

The above letter is the one you send to bring to the attention of the account holder that you intend to dispute the account on your credit report. You should then allow a reasonable amount of time to go by before sending them a follow up letter either letting them know they haven't replied and you will now go to the next step, or challenging any reply they send if it does not contain valid or relevant information.

Many creditors will understand the direction of your dispute, especially when they consider your wording specifically requesting information that ties you contractually to them in business to validate the account.

These companies will likely go ahead and close the account on their own to avoid being held liable for violating the Fair Credit Reporting Act and the Fair Debt Collection Practices Act and the steep financial consequences that could come from a lawsuit. For these companies, it is more practical to dismiss a $300 debt account that they only paid pennies on the dollar to purchase from the company you actually did business with, than to fight for the account and end up paying thousands of dollars to you in the long run.

For the companies who are determined to hold on to the account and try to force you to pay it, you have two choices. You can pay the account off after your first letter doesn't lead you to the results that you want. Or you can proceed to the next dispute letter to get the company to send you some verification tying you to the account. If they have sent you some evidence that does not tie you to the account, the following letter will be sufficient to send in.

Letter #2A.

Date
Your name
Your address
Name of company on your credit report
Address of company on your credit report
Re: Account # (as shown from company on your credit report)

To whom it may concern:

    This letter regarding account #_____, which you claim that I owe $_____.

Yet again, you have failed to provide me with a copy of any viable evidence, bearing my signature, showing the account is bring reported accurately.

Be advised that the description of the procedure used to determine the accuracy and completeness of the information is hereby requested.

Additionally, please provide the name, address and telephone number of each person who personally verified this alleged account, so that I can inquire about how they "verified" without providing any proof bearing my signature.

As per FTC opinion letter from the Attorney General, you should be aware that a printout of a bill or itemized document does not constitute verification.

I am again formally requesting a copy of any documents, bearing my signature, showing that I have a legally binding contractual obligation to pay you the alleged amount.

Be aware that I am making a final goodwill attempt to have you clear up this matter. The listed item is inaccurate and incomplete, and represents a very serious error in your reporting.

I am maintaining a careful record of my communications with you for the purpose of filing a complaint with the Consumer Financial Protection Bureau and the Attorney General's Office, should you continue non-compliance of federal laws under the Fair Debt Collection Practices Act, the Fair Credit Reporting Act, and the corresponding local state laws. I further remind you that you may be liable for your willful non-compliance.

Failure on your behalf to provide a copy of any alleged contract or other instrument bearing my signature may result in a small claims action against your company. I would be seeking a minimum of $1,000 in damages per violation for:

Defamation
Negligent Enablement of Identity Fraud
Violation of the Fair Debt Collection Practices Act (including but not limited to Section 807-8).
Violation of the Fair Credit Reporting Act (including but not limited to Section 623-b)
Please be aware that dependent upon your response, I may be detailing any potential issues with your company via an online public press release, including documentation of any potential small claims action. I am also including a copy of my complaint to the organizations below:

CC: Consumer Financial Protection Bureau
CC: Attorney General's Office
CC: Better Business Bureau

You will be required to appear in a court venue local to me, in order to defend yourself. My contact information is as follows:

Your name (printed NOT signed) Your address
Your last 4 of SSN

There are certain companies that will not answer your first dispute letter at all. After 30 days of not hearing any response from a creditor/collection agency, you will want to send the following letter.

Letter #2B

Date

Your name
Your address
Name of company on your credit report
Address of company on your credit report
Re: Account # (as shown from company on your credit report)

To whom it may concern:

This letter is in response to your recent claim regarding account, which you claim I owe you $_____

By not replying in a timely manner to my initial letter, which you received via certified mail on.   :_____

you have not only violated federal and state laws, but have also failed to provide me with a copy of any evidence, bearing my signature, showing the account is being reported accurately.

Be aware that I am making a final goodwill attempt to have you clear up this matter. The listed item is entirely inaccurate and incomplete, and represents a very serious error in your reporting.

I am maintaining a careful record of my communications with you for the purpose of filing a complaint with the Consumer Financial Protection Bureau and the Attorney General's Office, should you continue in your non-compliance of federal laws under the Fair Debt Collection Practices Act, the Fair Credit Reporting Act, and the corresponding local state laws. I further remind you that you may be liable for your willful non-compliance.

Failure on your behalf to provide a copy of any alleged contract or other instrument bearing my signature may result in a small claims action against you. In such action, I would be seeking a minimum of $1,000 in damages per violation for:

Defamation
   Negligent Enablement of Identity Fraud
   Violation of the Fair Debt Collection Practices Act (including but not limited to Section 807-8).
   Violation of the Fair Credit Reporting Act (including but not limited to Section 623-b)

Please be aware that dependent upon your response, I may be detailing any potential issues with your company via an online public press release, including documentation of any potential small claims action. I am also including a copy of my complaint to the organizations below:

CC: Consumer Financial Protection Bureau
CC: Attorney General's Office
CC: Better Business Bureau

You will be required to appear in a court venue local to me, in order to defend yourself. My contact information is as follows:

Your name (printed NOT signed)
Your address
Your last 4 of SSN

Sometimes, rarely but possible, you will dispute the collection accounts on your credit report and the collection agency doesn't answer you. Instead you end up receiving a response from the original creditor attempting to justify the debt. This is absolutely NOT acceptable.

In this case you would send the following dispute letter:

Letter #2C.

Date
Your name
Your address
Name of company on your credit report
Address of company on your credit report
Re: Account # (as shown from company on your credit report)

To whom it may concern:

On_____, I wrote to you requesting validation and an investigation into items that I believed were inaccurate. To date, I have not received any such validation. The only reply that I received from this matter was a letter from the original creditor _____, dated _____.
In my previous request directly to you I listed my reasons for disputing the information and requested validation.

Since this is my second request, I will also be sending a copy of this letter to the Federal Trade Commission notifying them that I have signed receipt for letters sent to you and you have not complied with my request. I regret that I am being forced to take such action.

Please note that on 3/20/2021 the CFPB released its Fair Debt Collection Practices Act Annual Report and it stated the following:

"The Bureau notes that one or more debt collectors continued collection activity despite not properly obtaining and mailing debt verification after a consumer exercised his or her 1692g rights. Specifically, the Bureau calls out the practice where debt collectors forwarded consumer debt validation requests to the relevant clients, who mailed responses directly to the consumers.

Section 809(b) of the FDCPA requires a debt collector, upon receipt of a written debt validation request from a consumer, to cease collection of the debt until IT (meaning the collection agency) obtains verification of the debt and mails it to the consumer. Examinations found that one or more debt collectors routinely failed to mail debt verifications before engaging in further collections activities.

Instead, one or more debt collectors forwarded consumer debt validation requests to the relevant clients, who mailed responses directly to consumers and debt collectors then continued collection activities on accounts in violation of section 809(b) of the FDCPA."

Failure on your behalf to provide a copy of any alleged contract or other instrument bearing my signature may result in a small claims action against your company. Therefore, either provide the requested information or cease your collection efforts and reporting of this account on my credit reports immediately.

Sincerely,

_____
Your Name (printed not signed)

My contact information is as follows:

Your name (printed NOT signed)
Your address
Your last 4 of SSN

A creditor/collection agency might respond with what they consider "proof" of your original signature and obligation to pay. You must wait until the 31st day from when they received your first letter, then check your credit report to make sure they have not marked the item as "disputed". If it is not marked as "disputed" in the comment section, we typically proceed ahead and send the following letter.

Letter #3.

Date
Your name
Your address
Name of company on your credit report
Address of company on your credit report
Re: Account # (as shown from company on your credit report)

To whom it may concern:

Upon further investigation, I have retained new copies of my credit reports, and noticed that you did not furnish the credit bureaus with the required disclosure, within the period required by law. You are required by federal law to place a "notice of dispute" on my account within 30 days of my dispute, which you are signed for on _____ showing you received it. I have retained a copy of your signature and date of receipt, as well as a time-stamped copy of my credit reports, showing that you have violated the Fair Credit Reporting Act, Section 6232(a)(3) and/or the Fair Debt Collection Practices Act Section 807(8) by not placing the disclosure within the required 30-day period.

Be aware that I am making a final goodwill attempt to have you clear up this matter. The listed item is entirely inaccurate and incomplete, and represents a very serious error in your reporting.

I am maintaining a careful record of my communications with you for the purpose of filing a complaint with the Consumer Financial Protection Bureau and the Attorney General's Office, should you continue in your non-compliance of federal law under the Fair Credit Reporting Act.

I further remind you that you may be liable for your willful non-compliance, as per FCRA 623(a) (3) — Responsibilities of furnishers of information to consumer reporting agencies [15 U.S.C. 1681S-2]

(3) Duty to provide notice of dispute. If the completeness or accuracy of any information furnished by any person to any consumer reporting agency is disputed to such person by a consumer, the person may not furnish the information to any consumer reporting agency without notice that such information is disputed by the consumer.

(B) Time of Notice (I) The notice required under subparagraph (A) shall be provided to the customer prior to, or no later than 30 days after, furnishing the negative information to a consumer reporting agency described in section 603 (p).

As you have violated federal law, by not properly providing the credit bureaus with proper notice within the required timeframe, and I have evidence of such, via certified mail receipts, you must now remove the item. Any other action (or inaction) on your behalf may result in a small claims action against your company. I would be seeking minimum of $1,000 in damages per violation for:

Defamation
   Negligent Enablement of Identity Fraud
   Violation of the Fair Debt Collection Practices Act (including but not limited to Section 807-8).
   Violation of the Fair Credit Reporting Act (including but not limited to Section 623-b)

Please be aware that dependent upon your response, I may be detailing any potential issues with your company via an online public press release, including documentation of any potential small claims action. I am also including a copy of my complaint to the organizations below:

CC: Consumer Financial Protection Bureau
CC: Attorney General's Office
CC: Better Business Bureau

You will be required to appear in a court venue local to me, in order to defend yourself. My contact information is as

Oh, My Credit!!

follows:

Your name (printed NOT signed)
Your address
Your last 4 of SSN

The above dispute letters will help you in your endeavors to improve your credit score. Keep in mind that some companies may not budge and you may have to pay those accounts off in order to see the information removed from your credit report. Although you may not want to pay the money, it will be your only option, so your best bet would be to go ahead and pay off the accounts that companies fight hard to keep. This is why I paid off the electric bill that showed up on my credit report after I first tried to dispute it.

Another thing that is important for you to know is what things on your credit report you should even put time into disputing. Some negative things on your credit report won't be worth your time and effort disputing because they will very shortly be falling off of your credit report on their own.

The vast majority of negative information stays on your credit report for 7 years. Missed payments, accounts that are sent to collection agencies, accounts consistently NOT being paid as agreed, and bankruptcies stay on your credit report for approximately 7 years.

NOTE: Some bankruptcies can stay on your credit report for as long as 7-10 years.

To figure out how long something will be on your credit report, look at the time when you FIRST missed a payment, not the date when the account went to collections. Your 7 years start counting on the date of your first missed delinquent payment. So, if you are fixing your credit right now and see some things on your credit report that are close to being 7 years old, you don't have to dispute them because they are going to fall off of your credit report on their own within a short time.

The easiest things to dispute on your credit report are:

Outdated accounts.
Inaccurate accounts that were late but now paid off.
Inaccurate late payments.
Inaccurate charge-offs and settled accounts.
Inaccurate authorized user accounts.
Accounts that do not belong to you.

The hardest things to dispute on your credit report:

Inaccurate new late payments of 30, 60, 90, and 120 days, and child support.
An inaccurate bankruptcy.
Inaccurate foreclosures and repossessions.
Inaccurate unpaid tax liens and judgments.
Inaccurate recent charge-offs and new collections.

If you have a 5 year old late payment deleted from your credit report, you can gain 10 points on your credit score. If you have a recent late payment deleted you can gain 100 points on your score. If you have a page of collections deleted you can gain 100 — 120 points on your score. So, do not underestimate the impact of successful disputes.

The most common and effective reasons to give for your dispute:

Outdated.
The account in question is not yours.
You have no record of being late.
A trade line displays the wrong amount.
The account number is incorrect.
The accounts are unverifiable.
The original creditor is wrong.
The charge-off date is inaccurate.
The date of last activity is wrong.
The credit limit is incorrect.
The status is wrong.
The high credit is wrong.
The charge-off amount is wrong.
The balance is wrong.
The items are questionable or misleading.
The accounts are erroneous.
Inaccurate or incorrect.

Review your credit report vigorously to see what items are good and bad, what items you should dispute, what items you should pay off, and what items are going to disappear from your report because of time. Nothing is as important as reviewing your credit report regularly, I cannot stress that enough. When I started building my credit I used creditkarma.com constantly to keep a consistent eye on my credit report, (Equifax and TransUnion). So, **CONSTANTLY CHECK YOUR CREDIT REPORT!!**

Regularly checking your Equifax credit report is an important step to ensure your information is accurate and complete. It also will help you confirm that any negative information falls off after the appropriate time period. You are entitled to a free copy of your credit reports every year from each of the 3 nationwide credit bureaus. You can do this by going to annualcreditreport.com. You can also create a myEquifax account to get 6 free Equifax credit reports each year. Additionally, you can click "Get my free credit score" on your myEquifax dashboard to enroll in Equifax Core Credit for a free monthly Equifax credit report.

CHAPTER FOUR
Inquiries: What they are and how they can affect you credit score.

There are two kinds of inquiries as it pertains to your credit report: **HARD** inquiries and **SOFT** inquiries. One kind can be harmful to your credit report and score while the other is harmless. Hard inquiries are potentially hurtful. Soft inquiries are harmless.

When you apply for any financing or credit and the lender checks your credit report as a part of the process in lending you the credit, or not lending it to you, this is called a hard inquiry. They are also known as "hard pulls" or "hard credit checks". They usually take place when you are applying for a mortgage, loan, or credit card.

A hard inquiry could lower your credit scores by a few points. Customarily, a single inquiry is unlikely to play a role in keeping you from getting approved for a loan or new credit card. And when you have a few hard inquiries on your credit report, the damage to your score will decrease and disappear even before the inquiry permanently drops from your credit report. Hard inquiries typically stay on your credit report for about 2 years.

This doesn't sound terrible, but, trust me, you have to

carefully manage your inquiries because they can add up and do some unnecessary damage on your score. Avoid applying for a lot of credit cards at the same time or even within the span of a few months. Multiple hard inquiries in a short period is a bad look to lenders. It suggests to them that you may be hard up for money and are recklessly applying for credit in desperation to get funds you may not be able to pay back. This makes a credit seeker look high risk. Because of this you need to spread out your credit card applications.

As a rule the negative effect of hard inquiries on your credit scores depends on your overall credit status. Adding one or two hard inquiries to your credit reports could shave a couple of points off your scores, but that's unlikely to have a huge detrimental impact. Just keep away from too many inquiries in a short timeframe. There can be exceptions when you are looking for specific types of loans, like student loans, mortgages, or car loans.

NOTE: Because of the shopping around that naturally goes into student loans, mortgages, and car loans, credit bureaus list them on your credit report differently from the way they list other inquiries. Credit card inquiries are listed individually, period. If you apply for 10 credit cards, you will have 10 hard inquiries showing up on your credit report for them. But with the other named loans, there is a 14 day grace period where your credit report will only reflect ONE hard inquiry for those that take place within that 14 day span. But the loan applications have to be in the same type. If you go to 10 auto dealerships within 14 days and each of them pull your credit report to see if you qualify for a loan from them, these inquiries will show up as ONE. The same thing goes for multiple hard inquiries for student loans, as

Oh, My Credit!!

well as multiple hard inquiries for mortgages. But, if you apply for a car loan, a mortgage, and a student loan, they will show up as THREE hard inquiries because they are different types of loans within the types that credit bureaus appoint the 14 day grace period to.

Some lenders have their own scoring models that allow for you to have more time to shop around with multiple loans of the same type, but I strongly suggest sticking to the 14 days period since you won't know what scoring model an individual lending company might be using. You don't want to get an additional hard inquiry because you assume that one lender is doing things the same another lender did.

Common hard inquiries are:

   Mortgage applications
   Auto loan applications
   Credit card applications
   Student loan applications
   Personal loan applications
   Apartment rental applications

Soft inquiries, also knowns as "soft pulls" or "soft credit checks" typically occur when a person or a company checks your credit as a part of a background check, such as takes place with some employers before they hire you. This also happens when ANYONE, BUSINESS OR OTHERWISE, checks your credit without your signed permission to see if you qualify for certain credit card offers or loans.

NOTE: Any checking of your credit done without your signature should not show up on your credit reports in a way that can be seen publicly upon credit checks. If they are listed at all, they will only be visible to YOU when you are viewing your own credit report. That is because soft inquiries are not connected to any specific application for new credit.

Soft inquiries won't affect your credit scores at all. If you are even unsure about how an inquiry will be classified, you should ask the company if the inquiry will be a hard or soft pull.

Common soft inquiries are:

Checking your own credit report
Prequalified credit card offers
Prequalified insurance quotes
Employment verification (background checks)

Remember to check your credit score on a regular basis

CHAPTER FIVE

Building credit: Different trade line transactions needed to boost your credit score

Trade lines are the accounts that show up on your credit report indicating a business transaction between you and any lender or other businesses that report your payments to the credit bureaus; Experian, TransUnion, and Equifax.

More thoroughly described, trade lines are records of consumer credit behavior. They show the activity and status of all credit accounts on your report. A trade line has the creditor's account name, the account number, and your payment status. The trade line will tell potential creditors whether you are paying your bills on time, late, or not at all. It also shows how much is owed on the account.

You want to accumulate as many good trade lines as possible and make sure that all the trade lines on your credit report are in good standing. These trade lines are what creditors look at to determine your credit worthiness. Trade lines are also a huge part of what the credit bureaus use to calculate your credit score.

By taking care of your financial responsibilities and making sure that your trade lines reflect that, you will put yourself in a position of having full leverage when it comes to obtaining credit and loans you need for any reason. When lenders look at your credit report and see how responsible you are they will be forced to compete for your business. Once you make it known that you are shopping around, they will immediately offer you attractive interest rates hoping to get you to choose them, not the other way around. Having a good credit score gives you a financial advantage that can be used to accomplish many things you would never even be able to try with poor credit.

There are four types of accounts in a trade line. Within each type are specific business transactions between you and a creditor. They are as follows:

Installment accounts:

Auto loans
Secured bank loans
Unsecured bank loans
Student loans
Any bills and rent accounts that report to credit bureaus

Revolving accounts:

Secured credit cards
Unsecured credit cards
Retail cards
Piggybacking / authorized user credit cards

Mortgages:

*Mortgages paid on time each month will help increase your credit score.

Trade lines are vital on your credit report and there are now a growing number of small businesses that focus on using the trade lines of clients with great credit to build the credit of other customers by way of selling/renting them temporary access to trade lines of the client with good credit, with his or her permission and shared benefit. This will be described a little more in Chapter Seven.

Now that you know what trade lines are and the significance of them on your credit report, I will show you how to utilize each of the biggest accounts on your trade line to boost your credit over a sustained amount of time or within a shorter period.

CHAPTER SIX

Secured and Unsecured bank loans

When you get to this level in your credit building journey, you will already have done your due diligence to know where your credit score is and what steps you need to take in proceeding. Building your credit is not a hard process, it's a tedious one. It requires your constant attention and your DELIBERATE taking of each step along the way. Nothing about building your credit should be taken for granted. All it will take is just a little bit of carelessness on your part to harm your credit again. Treat your credit like a plant that you have to constantly watch and water in order for it to grow.

Secured bank loans = bank loans that require you to have assets as collateral or money in your savings account to secure the loan.

Secured bank loans will have a big impact on your credit if it is low and you are aiming to build it up. This is because of the big increases that come from establishing the payment history with them and the benefits of paying these loans off on schedule. You can obtain secured loans like this from traditional banks or even from credit unions.

All you do to get a secured loan like this is open a checking and savings account with the bank or credit union, put money in your savings account, and then apply to get a secured loan using the funds in the savings account as collateral to secure the loan. The amount of the loan will be frozen in your savings account, meaning you won't be able to access it. A payment schedule will be established. As you make payments on the loan, the amount of each payment will be unfrozen in the savings account. This will continue to happen until you have paid off the loan in full. Being secured, these loans typically have great interest rates. Because you have furnished the amount of the loan before even getting the loan, you are, in essence, just paying a small amount by way of interest for the loan to have the great increase that will show up on your credit report for the transaction between you and the bank or credit union.

When shopping for banks to use the secured loan system of building credit, be sure to inquire about their process of issuing secured loans. This will keep you from being surprised after opening the accounts you need.

NOTE: You can speed up the process of building credit with secured loans by leveraging multiple secured loans at the same time. To do this, you simply get a secured loan at one bank, take the money you get from there and go to another bank repeating the process. Then you can take the money from the second bank and go to yet a third bank repeating the process again. In the end, you will have awesome credit at MULTIPLE brick and mortar financial institutions, giving you a great business relationship with them. And when these loan payments are reported, other financial institutions that you seek to deal with will be able to see that you are a great candidate to lend money or credit to.

You can realistically see a credit score increase of 50-100 points as a result of secured bank loans in good standing on your credit report. So, if you want to be bullish about this strategy all you have to do is utilize the game plan described in the above NOTE. And there are no limits to the amount of banks you can use this strategy with to get secured loans. It's your money, which means the banks or credit unions have absolutely 0% risk tied up into the transaction. As you make payments to unfreeze the money in your accounts, you are building excellent credit standing with these banks and an impressive track record for creditors to see.

The best approach to this strategy, regardless of how many banks or credit unions you use for this purpose, is to go through at least two full loans before taking the next step into unsecured loans. The more secured loans you go through and pay off on time and in full, the closer you will be to guaranteeing your ability to get the unsecured loans you later apply for at these same institutions.

After doing a few of these secured loans you will be able to apply for a loan on your signature at these banks and realistically receive it because they've already done business with you and view you as credit worthy.

Unsecured bank loans = bank loans that do NOT require you to have assets as collateral or money in your savings account to secure the loan.

Unsecured loans are the absolute biggest ticket items on

your credit report because it's not easy for anyone to just show up to a bank and walk out with a loan on their signature. The fact that you were deemed credit worthy enough to even get the loan works to your benefit on your credit, but only if you pay your bill on this loan on time every single month. Having a trade line that is an unsecured bank loan on your credit report will give you more nearly 100 points alone on your credit score. These kinds of trade lines are invaluable when you are advancing in building your credit.

The best thing about the unsecured bank loan is that you don't have to have anything backing it up, like property or other assets, or even money in your savings account. A bank or credit union that gives you an unsecured loan strictly because your credit report, coupled with your income, shows them you are good for it. It's a business transaction built on trust. This is the reason that interest rates on unsecured loans are typically much higher than that of secured loans. You get approved for unsecured loans because of who you have already demonstrated yourself to be in the financial world.

By managing your unsecured loan properly, meaning you make your loan payment on time every month, you will easily find yourself in the 720+ club on your credit score, if you are not already there. This is especially true if you make your payment on time for a few months and then pay off the loan in full. There is not a single trade line in the credit world that looks better on your credit report than a paid off bank loan, especially when it's a loan that is significant when calculated against your yearly income.

For example, if your income is $35,000 per year and you have a paid off bank loan on your credit report for a $1,000 unsecured loan, that will look good on your credit report simply because it's an unsecured loan. But, this loan is only 2.9% of your income, which doesn't stand out more than that. So, even though you will get the props for paying off the unsecured loan, it will be kept in perspective considering the amount of the loan compared to your income.

On the other hand, if your income is $35,000 per year and you have a paid off unsecured bank loan of $10,000 showing up on your credit report, that is a whole other animal altogether. This trade line will practically leap off of your credit report page with fireworks going off behind it. Not only is this a paid off unsecured loan, but the loan itself is a ridiculous 29% of your income. That percentage tells lenders that you are a top shelf candidate for their business. As a matter of fact, they will be clamoring for YOUR business.

No matter where your credit score is right now, the one thing you need to keep in mind on your credit building journey is that lenders are in the business of lending money to people like you and making a profit for themselves in the interest attached to the loan or credit they give you. Know this at all times so that you never become overwhelmed by the process, or start to give yourself self-defeating talk. If you take the steps in this book to build your credit, you will become such a valuable asset in the credit world that you will find early on that you are receiving unsolicited credit offers and loan offers that you don't even know what to do with because you have to vet the companies. Basically, when you start on a path like this it will get noticed. Whatever your credit building goal is, you can do that twice

Oh, My Credit!!

over because when your credit report shows you to be good for it there are limitless lenders who will climb over each other for your business.

CHAPTER SEVEN
Secured and Unsecured Credit Cards

Secured credit cards operate much the same as secured bank loans, as described in chapter 6. One difference is in the fact that, with secured bank loans, you will be given a certain fixed payment amount to make every month until the loan is completely paid off. With a secured credit card, you will control the amount you need to pay on it by the amount that you spend on the card every month.

Secured credit cards = credit cards that require you to furnish them with money up front in order to secure the line of credit. The limit on a secured credit card is equal to the amount of money you put on the card.

Because the secured credit card is backed by the money that you put onto it ahead of time, it is usually really easy to obtain them. You will want to manage your secured credit card the same way that you would manage an unsecured card because it is good practice being that getting to the unsecured level is your goal. Make small purchases with your card and make your payments on time every single month religiously. Because of the money that secures the credit card, you will never have to worry about not paying. Just be mindful about the rate at which you spend the money so that you can manage the balance on the card in a way that gives you the benefit of having an actual history making the payments on the card. Don't race through it.

NOTE: With unsecured credit cards, I suggest getting multiple cards. This won't be the same as getting multiple secured bank loans as described in the previous chapter because with secured bank loans you actually will have cash money in your account that can't be touch and cash in your hand that you can take to other banks to do the process again. But, with secured credit cards, you are putting money onto the card to determine the line of credit you will have, and payments will be made from there accordingly. There is no cash in hand to take to another credit card company for another secured credit card. You will have to apply again to another company for the new secured credit card. And you can do this as many times as you have the money on hand to furnish. In the end you will be making payments on the accounts and locking in great trade line entries onto your credit report.

Make sure that when you are shopping around for secured credit card lenders, you stay mindful of the fees that are involved with each company's process. Don't play yourself by taking on fees that aren't worth the deal just to get the card! Remember this deal is all about you using YOUR OWN MONEY to build your credit. Lenders in these secured credit card deals are winning all the way around the board because they aren't giving you anything, they're just collecting a profit from your desire to improve your credit. So, don't be pulled into steep fees. Shop carefully and shop smart. The best secured credit cards will be the bank issued cards that you can find at the biggest banking institutions in America.

> Bank of America
> Wells Fargo
> Capital One
> Orchard Bank
> New Millennium Bank First Premier Bank

To find an even bigger list of the best credit lending institutions to look at for secured credit cards, you can visit the following sites:

> creditcards.com
> creditcardscenter.com
> e-wisdom. com
> bankrate.com
> cardrating.com

A great thing about having multiple secured credit cards is that most companies have pretty similar rules with issuing lines of credit, need they be secured or unsecured. So, when you get to the point where you are ready to go to the next step, you will realistically be able to accomplish it with each company that you are in business with. This gives you multiple credit lending institutions who will take you seriously when you apply for unsecured credit cards with them.

Remember, in doing your due diligence, it is a must that you ask the following questions to any company you are even considering to use for a secured credit card:

> * Does your company report payments to all three credit bureaus?

* What are your credit card fees?
* At what point in the process will I qualify for an unsecured line of credit?

Unsecured credit cards = credit cards that do NOT require you to furnish them with money up front in order to secure the line of credit. The limit on an unsecured credit card is determined by the credit lending institution based on what they deem is a good risk based on your credit report.

When you have established a good enough relationship with the credit lending institutions to go after unsecured credit lines, you want to start small. As small as practical for you to get approved. Once you have the card (or cards if you are going for multiple lines) you want to use them diligently and wisely, maintaining a low balance by paying your bill every single month. I strongly advise you to have your bank checking account or a specific card set to make your payments through autopay every single month at least a week BEFORE your monthly payment due date. This will keep you ahead of schedule on your payments. Also, try to get in the habit of giving an extra payment on your account just in case any unexpected situation may happen outside of your control that puts you at risk of having a late payment.

Regardless to what your strategy is for avoiding late payments, you need to view late payments as the devil and avoid them at all times and at all costs. It would be a shame for you to work your ass off to build your credit and to watch your score rise with every step, only to then have it all come undone by a missed payment. Remember, creditors don't care about why a payment was late, they just see it as a scar on your credit report if it is there.

Your credit report should reflect at least 2 years of solid payment history with at least one small credit card, and one installment loan (like a bank loan), before you go after the major credit card from larger institutions. If you have followed just the steps already given you are well on your way to getting that done. Keep in mind that there are strategies for certain people to have things work at an even faster timeframe. These strategies, like authorized user accounts, piggy backing, cosigners, and trade line rentals are talked about more in Chapter 9 in this book.

The most important thing about any credit card you have is that you avoid debt. You need to make sure you are careful to not spend more during any month than you can afford to pay off in full when your bill is due. Leaving any remaining balance is counterproductive because when you have not paid the bill in full you automatically end up with interest charges for that on top of what you owe. High interest charges can potentially put you in a position to be in bad standing with your credit card payments, and challenge your understanding of your entire line of credit.

The amount of money you are charged for your card is called your Annual Percentage Rate, or APR. Some cards have a higher APR, as much as 24%. This means that if you have paid off your balance this month EXCEPT for $100, you now owe that $100 plus $24, for a total of $124 owed.

Further, if you only pay off the minimum amount due every month on your credit card, that amount will only go towards your interest from the previous month. So, in that event, your bill would look like this $100 (balance) + $24

Oh, My Credit!!

(APR) - $15 (minimum payment) = $109 (new balance). So, with a new balance of $109, if you repeat another minimum payment, you will end up with a bill of $109 (balance) + $26.16 (APR) - $15 minimum payment) = $120.16 Now you can see how paying a minimum amount can cause you to pay many times more for a credit line than the principal on the card. And it would take literally YEARS to pay off even a small credit line with this minimum payment strategy, ALWAYS pay off your total balance. When you buy something, pay for it at the end of the month, that's the whole purpose of credit being used to your benefit in the first place.

You don't want to max out your credit cards, either. Instead, use what those with the highest credit scores use as a foundation to keep them consistent. Most people with the highest credit scores only use up to 30% of their total line of credit every month. This shows that you have restraint and purpose with your spending. This is also the best approach to use to get your creditors to increase your lines of credit. If you are paying your balance every single month and your credit line is decreasing in a responsible way, the credit lender will not want you to pay all the line off and leave them for another company, or leave them and decide that you've had enough credit. So, when you are paying on time consistently, when your line gets really low, they are likely to simply offer you a generous increase on the credit line at an even better APR.

Managing your credit line usage rate is really important. If you spend your whole line, even if you pay off the balance in full, it's not going to look better than you would look by not having a balance at the end of the money and paying your bill on time. Try to stay within 30% of your credit line max. Let that be a rule.

CHAPTER EIGHT
Retail Credit Card/Lines of credit

Retail credit cards = Credit cards that are issued by specific businesses. These lines of credit are only usable with that particular business. e.g. A Macy's card is only good when used at Macy's.

Retail credit cards are much easier to apply for and receive than major credit cards are. This is because these cards are restricted to being used at the business that issued them and because the limits on them are usually low. The big benefit to having retail credit cards is that they are easier to get than major cards, but they show up on your credit report with the same great impact that the major credit card does. After you have paid on your retail credit card for a few months you can check your credit report and see how they look there and how they have increased your credit score.

These cards give you the ability to purchase merchandise at whatever business that issued them. You can buy that merchandise and later pay your monthly bill on it, so that you are getting the materials you need while also receiving the increase in your credit score.

Some stores are easier to apply for credit with. Most will

start you off with a really small limit. Don't spend the limit immediately just because you have the money to do so. Instead, you will want to spend 20% - 30% of the limit on the card every month for six months just so that you will have built a payment history on the card that will look much better to creditors than it would look if you rush to pay off the whole card in a shorter amount of time. The easiest retail credit cards to apply for are the following:

- Fingerhut
- JC Penny
- Macy's
- Lowes
- Home Depot
- Kay Jewelers
- Best Buy
- Fed Ex Kinko's
- Office Max
- Office Depot
- Sam's Club
- Staples
- Target
- Wal-Mart

These companies, especially Fingerhut, will give you a credit line right now and you can begin using them to build your credit. With Fingerhut, you will be given a small limit, around $300. When you begin to purchase things from them through their online catalog or their paper catalog that they mail to your residence, you will have a monthly bill to pay for those things. Paying them will immediately show up with the three credit bureaus and look good on your credit. The best thing about Fingerhut is that even though you may not have heard of them, or think of them as a small company, they have been around for decades and when you have an account with them and pay it off, they never close your account. Instead they will increase your credit limit. This will cause your credit report to have the payment history with them standing out more and more as time goes by.

This same thing can be done with businesses that offer "buy here pay here" credit lines, like Value City Furniture. They will let you have a line of credit with them and report your payments to the credit bureaus on your behalf. You will want to treat these accounts carefully because through them you can streamline yourself right into the major lines of credit you are ultimately looking for in the long run from major lenders.

If your credit report shows you paying consistently on 2 or 3 business lines of credit through retail credit cards or the "buy here pay here" option, your report will look good to the lenders you are trying to attract. Being able to keep these accounts on your report by paying them off over time and not rushing to use the whole limits will stand out as proof of how responsible you are as a borrower.

NOTE: When you get approved for lines of retail credit, you can do many creative things to put the lines of credit to work for you so that you do more than just get the benefits of making your monthly payments. You can try to make sure you get credit lines through companies that have products that you actually use, or you can simply make purchases through your line of credit and sell the merchandise you get and use the money to make payments on the line of credit and possibly have a profit at the end of the transaction. Or, you can buy things you will need to open up a small business that will bring you an extra income over the long run. Basically, you don't have to look at every financial windfall from the standpoint of a consumer.

Think of ways you can put money to work for you to make more money. Now put that same level of thinking into the lines of credit that you have at a store that you really don't have any personal use for. If you are creative with your searching you can surely find areas where you can make purchases that put a profit into your pocket while paying your retail credit bill in full every month.

CHAPTER NINE

Authorized Users/Piggybacking, Cosigners, and Trade line rentals

Authorized User, also known as piggybacking, accounts are those where you are included onto the already existing credit account that belongs to someone else. These can be awesome at building your credit in a really quick time. That is because these accounts have been opened for a long time already and when you get onto the account, all of that history on the account will show up on your credit report as if you have been a part of the account for the lifetime of it.

Here is how it works. You are in the process of building your own credit. You have a friend or family member who has great credit. You ask this friend to include you onto their credit card account as an authorized user. There will be a card issued in your name from the credit card company. It will be mailed to the address of the friend or family member who owns the account. The very next time the credit card company distributes information about the credit account to credit bureaus, you will have the entire credit history for the account showing up on your credit report.

There are pros and cons with using Authorized User accounts.

Pros: You will immediately be included onto the account at your friend or family member's request. The company won't have a problem with that because the account already exists. Being on the account means you will have access to the account just as the original owner of the account has. Because there is a lot of history on the account you will get that history on your own credit report and get the same benefits of that as the original owner of the account. There is no delay in reporting. As soon as you are included onto the account you will automatically be forwarded the history of the account, the age of the account, and the utilization rate (how much of the credit has been used). When credit issuers see your credit report, they will see a credit line with a long history showing up there and not know you just got onto the account.

Cons: If your friend or family member doesn't keep up with the payments on the account, or even if YOU are the one to use the account irresponsibly, that will reflect on both credit reports. Any late or missed payment by the holder of the account shows up against them and also against you.

As you can see, the pros outweigh the cons in Authorized User accounts. If you trust the person who you're approaching to be included on their credit account, this is the perfect way to rack up points really fast and build your credit score.

Oh, My Credit!!

A cosigner is somebody who has great credit and uses it to serve as a guarantor in order for you to get a credit line or loan that your credit isn't good enough for you to get on your own. This is a sensitive situation that also involves a lot of trust because the cosigner is trusting you to make your payments on your loan or credit account. If you don't they will be hit with the bad mark on their credit report along with you. They will be on the hook along with you to come up with the money to make the payment on the account if you pay late or not at all.

This is how cosigners work. You apply for a loan or a line of credit. You know ahead of time that you won't be able to get the loan on your own, so you reach out to somebody you know with good credit who trusts in you. During the application process, you have this person fill in the section designated for a cosigner. Now, after the lender runs a credit check on you, they will also run a credit check on your cosigner. If your credit isn't good enough, but the cosigner's is, you will be given the loan on the strength of the cosigner's credit. The cosigner understands that they are responsible for the account along with you.

Having a cosigner is a great way to build your credit because after you have taken care of your account and paid it off responsibly every month, not only will you be able to now get more loans or credit lines on your own credit, which will be good enough to do so now, but your cosigner will also get the credit for you paying on time and that will help their good credit look even better. Combined in the future, they will be able to help you get even higher loans or lines of credit and will trust you to pay on time because you already demonstrated an appreciation for your credit, and theirs.

Start with a small loan, not more than a few hundred dollars, and make for sure that you make every payment on time so that you reap the full benefits from having had a cosigner. By the end of a 12 month period, you will surely be able to get a loan from the exact same lender on your own.

Trade line rentals are a real thing that can have tremendous effect on your credit report, and your credit score. It works like this. You are building your credit and you want to get a loan or line of credit, but you need a bump on your credit report to get it done. Trade line renting, or for-profit piggybacking, happens when you PAY somebody, whether you know them or not, to become an authorized user on their account specifically so that they can reap the benefits of the long standing account. They get you included on their account and then destroy the credit card that is issued to you instead of giving it to you. That's because the only reason for the inclusion of you on the account is the good history being included on your credit report and you credit score.

Piggybacking companies started emerging in 2007. Trade line credit repair companies are useful if you do your homework and make sure the businesses you are dealing with are reputable. When used correctly and these companies do what they claim to do, your credit score will receive a really nice boost.

A 2010 Federal Reserve study found that thin credit files (meaning those with few trade lines reporting) had one of the largest score improvements from piggybacking/authorized user accounts, with score gains averaging between 45 — 64 points. Individuals with a short credit history such as two years or less also had a large score increase. Their average score increase was 22 points. There's significant benefits if you fall in either one of those categories or if your current score qualifies you as a subprime borrower.

Companies, and individuals who rent you trade lines will sign you up as an authorized user and protect themselves by:

* Not allowing the authorized user to have a credit card on the account.
* Monitoring the authorized user's credit score so that once that person's score increases, they can be removed from the account.

Some major credit card companies and banks have certain reporting language to alert lenders that information is including an authorized user on the account. But, almost ALL will report to all three credit bureaus the following information which benefits the holder of the account as well as the authorized user.

* Payment history
* Credit limit increases
* Age of the account

CHAPTER TEN
BONUS Chapter.... credit cards perks and potential pitfalls.

I could've put this information in Chapter 7 where credit cards are discussed. But, being that I didn't want to put anything in any of the chapters about specific credit building strategies that would be useful but distract from the direction of the chapters, I decided to include a couple of bonus chapters where I could include this information.

There are several perks involved with credit cards that a lot of us don't understand. When I got my first credit card, my lack of understanding of the perks caused me to pay them no attention. Then I began to get the benefits of them and immediately wanted to see for sure what perks I had in my other cards.

Because low risk credit consumers are in high demand and short supply, there is a raging competition between the credit card companies to attract as many of the available great credit consumers for themselves as they can get.

This competition is fought with interest rates and perks. If your credit is good enough you will find yourself getting the lowest interest rates on the market. Also, no matter

Oh, My Credit!!

what your credit is, if you are able to get ANY credit card, when you have had the card for a while and used it responsibly, there will be staggering perks that you can use. These perks will depend on your usage and can be very helpful.

When you watch TV and see a credit card commercial where Jennifer Garner or Samuel L. Jackson are running off a laundry list of perks you can get with Capital One, you may not understand all of what they're saying but if you have a Capital One card, you will see those perks popping up all over the place.

With all credit cards, their perks are usually referred to as "Rewards". They come in all kinds of common spending categories. Air miles, dining, gas, groceries, Global Entry or TSA PreCheck credit, and also added entertainment perks. Because the video streaming services market has become so competitive that the service providers have had to use unusual tactics to market themselves in attempts to put themselves ahead of the pack. This competition works to the benefit of credit card holders because so many of these service providers have partnered with credit providers to have their services used as an enticing incentive to get us, as customers, to choose their credit cards.

Certain credit cards — not only high end rewards cards but no-annual-fee options - are increasingly featuring streaming services among their merchant-specific cash back deals for consumers who choose them as lenders.

In July 2021 American Express listed offers of $20 off of $60 spent on the popular sports heavy service, FuboTV. This offer was good for up to three times. They also offered $25 back on $99 or more spent on an HBO Max annual subscription.

At several times throughout 2021, Amex and Chase had great cash-back deals involving Discovery +, Disney+, Paramount+, Peacock and Showtime. Some cards even go the extra mile by offering their own credits and bonuses for streaming expenses.

One thing credit issuers like about the relationship between themselves and streaming service providers is that the services already have built in limits of their own of how much people can spend there.

Chase's Freedom Flex made streaming one of its categories, again, that qualified for their 5% cash back for customers who opted in during the final quarter of 2021.

Because streaming services are easy and convenient for consumers to use due to their not imposing contracts to lock users into long term deals the way that cable TV services are still doing, we can all take advantage of these discounts and freebies to binge-watch whatever shows and movies we want and then cancel the service when the promotional time is up.

When you build up your credit to where you can get the biggest of the major cards that offer the craziest perks you will get benefits that you won't even believe until you see them on paper. That's why qualifying for these bigger cards require a higher credit score, between 800 and 850.

The Centurion Card from American Express (Black Card), is the Holy Grail of credit cards. One of the big reasons that this Black Card is so coveted is because of the exclusivity that comes with owning one, and because of just some of the perks.

With the Centurion Card, you get:

A 24/7 personal concierge
Access to Amex Centurion lounges
Delta SkyMiles Platinum Medallion status
Complimentary TSA Pre-check or Global Entry fee credit
And more....

With the Mastercard Black Card you get:

Lower fees than the Centurion Card's $10,000 initiation fee and $5,000 annual membership fee
You don't need an invite to apply (as you have to have with Centurion Card)
Luxury Concierge service
Annual airline travel credit of $100
An up to $100 application credit for TSA PreCheck or Global Entry
1.5% cash back on ALL purchases
The ability to redeem your points for 2 cents each towards airfare airline redemption with no blackout dates
And more....

With the JP Morgan Reserve Card you get:

Although it's invite only, this card has low annual fee, $595 per year.
An annual $300 travel credit
Invitations to exclusive events
Priority Pass lounge access

Up to a $100 statement credit for TSA PreCheck or Global Entry and more...

Although it is still impressive and attention grabbing when you slap down a Black Card onto the table to pay the tab for dinner, there is a card that gives you even more perks.

One of the best valued credit cards on the market is the American Express Platinum Card. **With the Amex Platinum Card you get:**

Intro offer of a whopping 100,000 membership rewards points after you spend $6,000 within your first 6 months of owning the card.

Low annual fees, $695 per year.

10x points on all eligible purchases on the Card at restaurants worldwide and when you shop small in the USA, on up to $25,000 in combined purchases within first 6 months of membership.

5 points per dollar on airfare (booked either directly with the airline or through Amex travel)

5x points on up to $500,000 on these purchases per calendar year

5 points per dollar on prepaid hotels booked with Amex Express Travel

1 point per dollar on everything else!

Up to $200 annual Amex Platinum airline credit for incidental expenses on your selected airline

Up to $200 in Uber credits per calendar year (for service

in the USA)

Up to $100 in credit for Saks Fifth Avenue

Global Entry or TSA PreCheck application fee credit up to $100

Then, there is the Chase Sapphire Reserve. It's most comparable to the JP Morgan Reserve Card. **With the Chase Sapphire Reserve Card you get:**

Earn 60,000 bonus points after you spend $4,000 in the first three months the day your account is opened.

3 Chase points per dollar on all travel

3 Chase points per dollar on dining

1 Chase point for everything else

Annual $300 travel credit

Up to two years of DoorDash DashPass membership

Premium Priority Pass membership

Those are examples of credit card perks and just a fraction of some of the cards that have the best packages of these benefits. Basically, don't just look at your credit card as a credit building tool. You have worked hard to get it, so take a hard look at the rewards and perks that your card carries and use the HELL out of them. **THEY ARE YOURS!!**

Potential pitfalls that come with owning a credit card:

Identity theft

Data breaches
Credit card fraud
Mortgage fraud
Or any combination of the above pitfalls.

In identity theft, a thief steals your identity for the purpose of using it to commit a crime or to sell your identity to somebody else who plans to commit a crime with it. Being victimized by identity theft involves someone stealing your personal information, such as your Social Security number, address, health insurance information or job history. Sometimes victims of identity theft don't discover the unfortunate situation until months, or even years, after the fact.

Data breaches describe what happens when a hacker uses cyber space to criminally break into a business's sensitive information for the purpose of gaining access to the personal and financial information of the business's customers. This is also called "phishing" The purpose of these break-ins can be two-fold. The hackers either want to sell your personal and financial information to identity thieves, or the hackers want to lock the business out of being able to have and control the information and ransom the information and files back to the business for a large amount of money.

Credit card fraud can happen a lot of different ways, all devastating to you. Somebody can use a skimmer to duplicate your credit card. Someone can also steal your identity and open a bunch of credit cards in your name.

Mortgage fraud can happen in a host of ways. One way that can affect you is when somebody uses your identity to purchase a mortgage.

Oh, My Credit!!

If left unchecked, any of these crimes can wreak havoc on your credit report and your credit score. Because you are on a mission to build your credit, you should be able to do so without the headache or negative energy involved in worrying about whether your identity is intact, or worrying about whether a thief has breached the data of any of the many businesses you deal with in your everyday life. The only way to avoid these worries is to know how to protect yourself and simply DO it.

According to the Justice Department, an estimated 16.6 million people experienced identity theft at least once in 2012. An estimated 7.7 million people within that group reported use of a credit card.

When it comes to credit card fraud, the credit card company is usually the first to let you know something is up. Credit card companies have units devoted to monitoring and detecting any potential signs of fraud. If your credit card charges maintain a certain pattern and then it suddenly experiences huge charges, this would be something that gets the company's attention. And they will promptly get yours. If you are not alerted, you might eventually realize that a credit card of yours is missing or a credit card bill is inaccurate. Checking a credit report or applying for a loan or a new job might lead to the first warnings of something being wrong.

The sooner you alert the credit card company, or any other business, about fraud on your account, the quicker you have it on record and you can then work to get it remedied so that you don't get stuck with the bill. If you lose a credit card, you should immediately notify the company about it. Federal law limits the liability if a card is stolen, but liability may depend on how quickly the loss or theft is reported.

It can take years to erase the damage brought by these crimes. The process is strenuous, meticulous, and involves a lot of different agencies working together. Law enforcement. Insurance companies. Financial institutions. During the process of you getting to the bottom of these crimes against you, it's going to take you a while to be able to access your own credit, your interest rates may skyrocket, late charges and delinquencies will accumulate. Things like finding a new job, or acquiring or maintaining health insurance may be negatively impacted.

Protect yourself ahead of time to avoid these inconveniences!!

Acquiring identity theft protection is easy. All you have to do is Google the topic and you will see the top providers of this service and be able to make up your mind on which company best suits what you are looking for. This is not something you should consider doing, it's something you MUST do. I can't emphasize it enough. It's better to protect yourself and your name and your credit history and know you are safe, than to assume you are secured and learn the hard way that you are not.

These Identity Protection companies offer all kinds of services to protect you. This includes alerting you any time your social security number is being used to obtain any kind of financial movement. They will also alert you to any excessive spending on your credit card. They will alert you to any attempt to gain a mortgage in your name. This alert is useful, and you can see it for yourself when you apply for something like a credit card and really soon thereafter there is an alert sent to your phone and email asking you to verify that it is indeed you doing the applying.

Another great way to protect yourself is by activating a Credit Freeze on yourself. A credit freeze, also known as a security freeze, lets you shut down your credit report and keeping your credit score from being released. This protects you because every financial institution that lends money or lines of credit absolutely DEMAND to see your credit report as well as your credit score. So, if you have a credit freeze on yourself, then no new accounts can be opened in your name.

A credit freeze does NOT affect your credit score, and they are free. The only cost is in the effort that you have to put forth to manage the freeze, putting it on when you are not doing anything with your credit, but taking it back off when you are about to apply for any kind of financing or health insurance. After you gain any of the credit accounts you are looking for, you have to then put the freeze back on.

To place a credit freeze on yourself, you must contact each credit reporting agency directly. Instructions are on the company websites to let you know what you need to do in order to get the credit freeze accomplished.

Equifax: equifax.com
Experian: Experian.com
TransUnion: transunion.com

When you set a credit freeze, you will select or be given a Personal Identification Number (PIN) that you will always need in order to activate or pause the freeze. You have to put that PIN number in a place where you can always get to it in the event that you don't remember it off hand. That way you won't ever have to go through the hassle involved with resetting the PIN. When getting the freeze started so that you can get your PIN, be prepared to give information like your Social Security number, name, address, date of birth, and other personal information. This is strictly for the purpose of the company making sure it is indeed you who are affecting your credit file with something as consequential as a freeze.

A credit freeze involves three actions: You can add, lift, or remove a credit freeze.

Adding the freeze means placing a freeze on your credit so that nobody can access it. Lifting means temporarily removing the freeze so you can apply for credit. Removing a freeze permanently takes the freeze off of your credit.

Your Pin lets you select what to do with your credit freeze and when to do it. When you are doing nothing in terms of getting new credit or loans, or anything else that will require your credit report to be scrutinized, you will need to have your credit freeze **added**. When you are applying for something that requires your credit report like getting a car loan, a mortgage, renting a car or an apartment, signing up for a new cell phone plan, applying for new utilities, applying for any kind of credit or credit cards, or even getting certain kinds of jobs where employers check your credit, you will need to first lift the freeze. You can add it back when you are done looking at your credit report in these new procedures.

A big plus with the credit freeze in protecting you from fraud is in the fact that you **can actually submit a request**

with all three credit bureaus to lift your credit freeze for a specific company for a specific timeframe. This means you can put a credit freeze on your whole credit file and selectively lift it when you are applying for something that requires a credit check. The best way to go about lifting the credit freeze is by phone or online. That way the lift will be completed in a matter of an hour or so.

Things to remember about your credit freeze to help you maneuver it to your needs are:

* Credit freezes do not affect your credit. Keep paying your bills and the points will keep going up.
* Credit freezes do not apply to **current credit accounts**. These creditors can still access your credit report because they are already on your credit file.
* Under certain circumstances, certain government agencies may still be able to gain access to your credit file. But, they will need a search warrant, court order, or subpoena.
* Credit freezes do not prevent you from obtaining your free annual credit report.
* Credit freezes do not keep you from gaining new credit, although you will need to lift the freeze in order to do so.
* Credit freezes do not prevent a thief from making charges to your existing accounts. You still have to monitor your bank, credit card and insurance statements for anything that looks fraudulent that you didn't do.

A credit freeze is extremely valuable and can help you avoid being a victim of fraud if you are discovering that you are a victim of identity theft. The freeze prevents opening new lines of credit because lenders check your credit file to see you credit worthiness. A freeze keeps them from being able to make that credit check, and, in turn, prevents a fraudster from victimizing you.

Because credit freezes are so affective in protecting you from the potential fraud that comes with identity theft, I strongly advise you to get a credit freeze. I also advise you to get **identity theft protection** for your existing accounts and all personal information, that way the identity theft protection will cover you when somebody tries to access your existing accounts and use them in a way that is outside of what you normally do or open new accounts using your personal information, while your credit freeze will protect your entire credit file from being accessed by anybody that you don't specifically give access to by temporarily lifting the freeze specifically for them.

Whether you decide to get a credit freeze or not, it's smart to take all steps available to help protect yourself against identity theft. Identity theft is a crime that grows exponentially year by year, and if you are paying attention, you will see that a large number of big companies who are victims of data breaches through ransomware are companies that you use yourself or millions of other people use. This puts your vital information in the hands of crooks who want to use your shit to commit fraud. And that fraud can DESTROY your credit, and even your personal life if you don't protect yourself against it ahead of time.

It's just that simple.

CHAPTER ELEVEN

BONUS Chapter.... other interesting credit facts to know.

In addition to all of the valuable information that you have already seen if you have read this far into the book, there are other bits of information that can also be helpful in your credit building journey. Below I'm going to list a lot of different things that are important to know just in case you are dealing in some of these areas. That way you know how to take full advantage of the options you have at your disposal.

So, without any buildup, I'm going to get right into these topics and usable points for you to be aware of.

The payday loan BAD myth

It is true that on their face, payday loans are designed for the purpose of raking you through the coals with extremely high interest rates, usually 15%. This is especially true when considering these loans are short term, usually a week or so until your next paycheck, and they are usually pushed towards people who are not making a lot of money anyway. Those bad things are very real and very consequential because if a payday loan is mismanaged you could wind up paying it off for years with an interest rate that costs you thousands of dollars. Because of that, using these kinds of payday loans are typically not even thought about. But, don't be so quick to write off these companies because if you use one of them that requires a credit check, you will be able to use it to your benefit. Basically you'll be using this payday loan to get "Paid as Agreed" on your credit report. The interest is high, but in the long run, it would be worth it. So, if you want to dish out $15 for every $100 of the loan (usually these loans max out as $500) to get instant points, it's not a bad idea.

You go to one of these payday loan companies that check your credit. After you meet their low credit requirements, they will give you a loan right on the spot. You can either pay the loan back right away on the due date, or you can utilize the monthly payment strategy and make payments on it that way. As you make the payments, the company will report it to the credit bureaus, giving you an installment loan on your credit report that looks great to FICO and will show up on your credit score.

Credit builder loans

If you are rebuilding your credit, using credit builder loans can be very valuable. These are loans that you get from a credit union. They lend you money that is then deposited into a CD (certificate of deposit). You make payments on the loan and the credit union reports these payments to the credit bureaus. After you pay off the total loan, you get the CD and have a better credit score through another "Paid as Agreed" installment loan on your credit report. The big benefit to this program that makes it different from a secured loan, is that with a credit builder loan you don't have to put any money up to get the loan. The money from the loan is set aside for you in a CD and you pay it off monthly like a regular loan until it's paid off. At the end of the usually 12 month period, you have already gotten the benefits of getting this loan onto your credit report and also having the points showing up.

Buying a car

Most major cities have car dealers, new and used, who offer bad credit auto loans. Buy here pay here, etc... They are convenient if your credit is not up to par and you are trying to get around. These loans don't come with a lot of red tape, but they can be expensive. You may have to make a large down payment and then take on a high interest rate over the life of the loan.

Before you sign any contract, make sure the dealer reports your payment history to the credit bureaus. That should be the first question you even ask the auto dealer. Many used car dealers will finance you with no credit as long as you have a good job they can verify along with the willingness to make a down payment on the car.

Purchasing a house with no credit or poor credit

Most banks will not lend money to you early in your credit building journey. That is just a fact, and an understandable one, Banks are in the business of lending money to low risk people who can and will likely pay the loan back. Because you're just in the beginning of building your credit, banks will not give you an unsecured loan. You can easily get a secured loan being that you put your own money up in a savings account to back the loan. But when you are looking for a home loan, it's an unsecured loan, by way of a mortgage that you need. This is going to be a problem that you can only fix with time.

Unless you go another route.

There are two ways you can buy a house with poor credit or no credit. The first way is buying owner-financed homes. This is where the homeowner sells you the house and finances it themselves. They don't run your credit, they simply draw up an agreement for the monthly payments you will pay for the house along with whatever down payment they require, and then you move in and make the payments until you own the house outright. If you default on the agreement, the homeowner can kick you out of the house and the money you put into it will be gone, possibly with the exception of some of the down payment. In this kind of deal, the homeowner is acting as the bank.

Then, there is the second kind of home purchase. You can rent to own a house. If you Google "rent to own homes in-" and put your city at the back of it, you will see hundreds, and even THOUSANDS, of rent to own homes right where you live or where you are planning to move. These are great opportunities if you have a good paying job and money to put down on a house. With your large down payment, you can get a lease purchase agreement with the owner of the house. In this contract, you are agreeing to pay the owner monthly payments for up to two years. When the two years term of the agreement is over, you will then have the option of buying the home or moving out of it. If you decide to buy the house, your credit will be great by this time, which will give you the ability to go back to the bank for a traditional mortgage loan. If you are a hustling type of business person, you may even have the money on your own to buy the house for yourself and own it outright without any outside financing.

So, if you want to buy a house and your credit is not high enough to get a mortgage, don't just give in. It's easy to buy a house from **owner-financers** and especially from the **rent to own** route.

Don't close old accounts

Closing old credit accounts are never a good idea. It will actually hurt you more than it helps you. It's like sweeping money off your kitchen table into the trash can. Your FICO score is based greatly on the trade line accounts you have on your credit report. The older your paid accounts are on your report, the better you look. When you close an old account you are erasing everything about that account from your report, including the age of that account. This hurts you by making your credit file younger than it was before you closed the account. So, don't do it. As a matter of fact, your goal should be to keep your accounts as long as you can. This is why having so many credit cards are not a good idea. 3-5 is seen as good. If you maintain 3-5 credit cards for 5 years, but your friend gets multiple new cards every year and closes the earlier ones to avoid cluttering his credit report, whose credit is going to be reflected better? YOURS. That's because you the same accounts on your report the whole 5 years and they are all showing as "Up-to-date", whereas your friend has a lot of NEW accounts showing as "Up-to-date". The age of your accounts show you to be more responsible over a longer period of time, and that is what building your credit is all about.

Instead of owning a gang of credit cards, get 3-5 of them and maintain your payments on them every month so companies will continue to increase your limit. Let that be your goal, getting new credit limits on the 3-5 credit cards you already have instead of getting new cards. Keeping a few credit cards for multiple years and having them all paid up looks great on your credit report in a way that is only matched or beat by multiple paid off installment loans.

Getting a credit increase

Getting your creditor to raise your limit will help you keep your account open, and it will also reduce your balance if you are close to using your limit. This will help put a few more points on your score by improving your usage rate. It will also give you a higher credit limit without having to go out and apply for another credit card to get access to more credit. This is yet another thing to remember about your credit card accounts that you can use to your advantage to get the maximum benefits of owning the card.

Re-aging delinquent accounts

If you have a late payment and want to have your account showing up as "Up-to-date", you can ask your creditor to re-age the account so that it shows up that way. When this happens, it's like the late payment never happened. There is a process for this, but your creditor will explain that to you when you apply for this status on the account. The Federal Financial Institutions Examination Council (FFIEC) establishes the qualification process for you to be eligible to re-age an account. A part of the process is you demonstrating a desire and capability to repay the debt on the account.

Use Experian Boost

Experian Boost is a free service offered by the credit bureau, Experian, to help you build your credit with things you do normally every month. Go to Experian.com and look up how you can use Experian Boost to include all kinds of payments you already make onto your credit report. They will help you include things like on-time utilities, cell phone, and even your Netflix payments on your report and have them included in your score. Although, you will get just a few points here, it can be enough to take your credit score from "fair" to "good". There is no such thing as too many ways to increase your credit score. Keep that in mind.

RentTrack and PayYourRent services

Services like RentTrack and PayYourRent will allow you to have your rent payments included onto your credit report. Sign up for one of these services, along with your landlord. For a fee, these programs will link your bank account with your credit report to share your rent payment history there. Renting is already a difficult thing to accept after you realize that you are paying money that you can't ever get back and it's not giving you any ownership or equity. At least you now know you can use your rent payments towards building your credit

CHAPTER TWELVE

BONUS Important fact: What it's going to take to fix wealth gap

In credit, as well as every other aspect of financial literacy in America, Black people are lagging behind. As a matter of fact, when it comes to retirement planning and investing, Americans as a whole are not properly equipped with financial education and tools needed to make good and sound financial decisions. This is because, in America, most states don't have any requirements for financial literacy classes for high school students. Any time there is a problem that affects all Americans, it is exacerbated among the Black population.

According to the Council for Economic Education, up to 2020 only 21 states required high schools to teach financial literacy, and only 25 states required a high school economics course. This means, there are literally millions of high school students graduating every single year and moving out into the world without any knowledge of managing money. They know nothing about leases, credit, opening and maintaining a bank account, the details of auto loans, student loans and other debt, what the federal minimum wage is and how it's close to impossible to maintain a living with $7.25, the details of percentage rates regarding home loans, or how to keep a budget or save for retirement.

On financial literacy instruction, only 17 states got an "A" or a "B". 35 states got a "C" or lower. To give you the significance of these numbers, consider this: The USA ranks only 14th in the world for the percentage of financially literate adults with a rate of just 57%. This, from the greatest nation on earth. The nation that has access to everything imaginable on earth. For some reason, our politicians have no problem with these numbers. We can all suspect that the people in charge of making the rules ignore numbers like these because they are themselves a part of the 1% of people who have and control practically all of the wealth. But that knowledge should not stop us from individually taking it upon ourselves to get the information we need and using it to better our own lives and even sharing that information with other people so they too can see that they can do it.

The best thing we can do is train our kids young, **VERY** young, to understand money and credit. There are a host of things we can put to work to help us teach our kids about the importance of money and how to properly manage it. We can get games online that are centered on finances. We can use real life situations to consistently involve our kids in the process of money moving around. The next time you are at the store with your young kid, you can do something as small but intriguing to them as handing them the credit card to pay at the register and having the clerk talk to them as if they are the one buying the groceries, even giving them the receipt. And sit down with them at home to explain what everything is on the receipt, showing them the prices and where the items are as you put them up together. Since the beginning of time kids have always been interested in what adults. This is why little kids like to play with toy cash registers and credit cards, because they see adults, mainly men, with them. It's why little girls like to play with baby dolls, because they see adults, mainly women, with them.

So, if you present finances to your children, it won't be hard at all to capture their interest in finances. You could get them to latch onto economics and budgets with nearly the same attitude they have about those toy registers and credit cards if you go about it the right way.

Your older kids would be honored to learn finances, especially if you are greasing their palms along the way and letting them know what they're supposed to have at a later date to have them show you how they plan to budget. You could give them books, have them look up the topic online for real homework, and you can have them come along with you when you are taking care of certain kinds of business. Have them watch you pay bills or even listen in on customer service calls to take care of things.

There are several things you can do for your kids to have them financially literate before they graduate high school. In doing this, you will be doing your kids a tremendous service and giving them a big advantage that nearly NONE of their peers have.

Financial literacy should be seen as the same as teaching a kid his or her ABCs. Anything less is questionable parenting, I'm sorry to be so frank but it's true. And all of us have been guilty of it. Young adults are right now wasting money like crazy, or making bad investments that make no sense because they never had the proper understanding of money before they became adults.

CHAPTER THIRTEEN

Conclusion, Personal story and encouragement from the Author

Back when I first started on my credit building journey, I got my first credit card with the help of a friend who allowed me to be an authorized user on their account. My goal was to put forth the effort to get some stuff cleaned off of my credit report. I had business ideas I wanted to indulge in that required me to have access to credit, but my credit at the time was certainly not good enough to get any credit on my own.

I didn't really know much about credit at the time, I just thought that you could apply for a credit card, get it and use it until there was nothing left on it to use. Then, you could get another one. I was wrong all the way on that thinking.

When I did learn things about credit, I found that a lot of the things I had already done in my past financial dealings were more helpful to me than I realized at the time. For instance, I bought multiple cars and maintained my payments on them until I paid them all the way off. This stood out on my credit report down the road. I had a Value City Furniture credit line of $3,000 that I paid off in full.

That also made my payment history on my credit report look really good.

Being on my friend's credit account allowed me to get points for the credit card being paid off on time. When all of these good things were combined on my report, I had a decent score going, especially since I was just now getting interested at all in my credit.

There were also some dings on my credit report from a few bills that I hadn't paid off in full that showed up there. They were scars that I didn't want so I had them handled to clean up my credit report.

Before long, I became hooked on building credit. Seeing how far you could go if you only put the effort in encouraged me to take full advantage of every opportunity that came my way that I could use to build my credit. There was not a time when I let something get by me.

Because I was just getting started, I was an avid user of creditkarma.com. I found it to be extremely useful, so I have used it for years. I use it because it is very important to constantly look at your credit report to see what is there and to fix anything that is not attractive to your FICO scoring. This so important because if you don't keep yourself aware of the information on your credit report, you could be operating in the blind without knowing what is on your credit report. If you don't know what's there, you won't know what you have to clean up.

I was nearly obsessed with fixing my credit to the point that when all was said and done I had paid off some credit cards, cleared all unattractive marks off of my credit report, maintained a great payment history with my current open credit accounts, and paid all my bills on time.

Oh, My Credit!!

Over the years, I have made a lot of money. But, while I was making so much money, I was moving with the same attitude that many young people move with. *As long as I got money, that's all that matters. I can get anything I want.* With that attitude, I found myself just flat out wasting good money on bullshit when I could've used it building my credit or any host of other constructive ways. I learned the hard way over those years that cash money does not compare **AT ALL** to a great credit score. That's a truth that many people still don't know because they haven't been in the position to see it firsthand like I have.

Let's say there's two people looking to buy homes for $250,000. Person one has bad credit and is denied a mortgage loan. Person two has great credit and is approved for a low interest mortgage loan. Person one will have to pay $250,000 cash for the property, which will lower their available cash on hand. Person two will only have to make a down payment which could be around 5%-20% of the home price so around $12,500-$50,000 and then make monthly payments of around $1,500. This leaves person 2 with more available cash on hand if the home needs unexpected repairs of if the owner wants to do updates to increase the value. Having good credit and properly managing it can give you greater financial options.

I could go all day long giving examples and analogies to emphasize how much more important credit is than cash, but I think that just this one was good enough to at least get your head nodding seeing how much sense this concept makes.

I used to blow money and get it right back nearly immediately just by hustling in business. That's not how credit works. If you make moves that blow your credit, it could take you YEARS to be able to fix the damage. And then you would have to start all the way over rebuilding it again.

Because I have worked so hard to get my credit score to 760, I take good care of it. I don't want anything to hurt my credit so I'm extra careful about what I do with my credit file.

1 break my neck to pay my bills on time. This is made easier for me because I am a firm believer in autopay wherever I can apply it. I also pay some accounts ahead by a payment or two so that I'm covered in the event of any kind of emergency that could cause me to not be able to pay on time in the next upcoming month. I look into what a credit card is all about before I apply for it because some may want different things that I'm not willing to give up, or want me to pay too much interest just to get a high limit. And I continue to check my credit report regularly in order to stay updated on every piece of movement there.

I'm so used to doing all of this that it's programed in me now. I don't play around with my credit. I am on a mission to get to 850 so I do everything in my own power to make that happen. That includes having identity theft protection and a credit freeze that I utilize strategically. I am keeping my credit freeze long term, so when I get ready to apply for a new line of credit or a loan, or anything else that I have to get a credit check to get, I simply log on to the credit bureaus and temporarily lift the credit freeze ONLY for the company that I'm applying to for credit. When they do what they have to do and get my credit report, I add the credit freeze right back on there in full.

Oh, My Credit!!

I decided to share all of this information with you because I walked the walk with building my credit and got to see what works and what doesn't. What ideas are good, and what ideas are stupid. Basically, I went from being a person who didn't know much at all about credit, to being one who learned so much about it over the years that I built my own score up to 760 (and counting), and I know for a fact that within a year I will be beyond the 800 range.

There is no better feeling than being able to know that you have built your credit up and when you are in need of something, like financing you can use for a business idea, you can get it without any question because you are seen as a great risk to invest in. I feel good every time I apply for something and not only do I get it, but I'm constantly being bombarded with offers from other lenders who want my business.

If you take the steps in this book, you too can have a credit score of 760 and be on your way beyond 800. All it takes is that first step, and that is truly WANTING to build your credit.

ABOUT THE AUTHOR

Cornelius Edrington, Author of OH My Credit, served 12 years in the federal correction institution. After reviewing my credit, I had to do something about it. I started reading books about credit and I trained myself on how to build and dispute things on my credit until I had a 700 plus credit score. Please know that this wasn't an easy task, as I was faced with a lot of ups and downs. Finally, everything started working to my benefit. Now I am in a position to improve my life and the life of my loved ones. I plan on touring with my book as soon as I'm released.

I look forward to seeing my readers soon.

Oh, My Credit!!

Order Form

Make **Money Orders** PayableTo:

Spect Publishing LLC
PO Box 929
West Chester, OH 45071

Ship To:	QTY	Available Publications	Price

Name: _____
Address: _____
City: _____ State: _____ Zip: _____

For Shipping and Handling: Add $3.75 for 1st Book. Add $1.75 for each additional book. All books are also available on Amazon and Kindle. All titles coming soon, also can be pre-ordered.

We Can Help You Self-Publish Your Book
You're The Publisher and We're Your Legs!
We Offer Editing For An Extra Fee, and Highly Suggest It, If Waved, We Print What You Submit!

We are not your publisher, but we will help you self-publish your book.

Ask About our Payment Plans
Contact
Crystal Perkins, MHR
Essence Magazine Bestseller
PO BOX 8044 / Edmond – OK 73083
www.crystellpublications.com
(405) 414-3991

Plan 1-A 190 - 250 pgs. $699.00   Plan 1-B 150 -180 pgs. $674.00
Plan 1-C 70 - 145pgs $625.00

2 (Publisher/Printer) Proofs, Correspondence, 3 books, Manuscript Scan and Conversion, Typeset, Masters, Custom Cover, ISBN, Promo in Mink, 2 issues of Mink Magazine, Consultation, POD uploads. 1 Week of E-blast to a reading population of over 5000 readers, book clubs, and bookstores, The Authors Guide to Understanding The POD, and writing Tips, and a review snippet along with a professional query letter will be sent to our top 4 distributors in an attempt to have your book shelved in their bookstores or distributed to potential book vendors. After the query is sent, if interested in your book, distributors will contact you or your outside rep to discuss shipment of books, and fees.

Plan 2-A 190 - 250 pgs. $645.00   Plan 2-B 150 -180 pgs. $600.00
Plan 2-C 70 - 145pgs $550.00

1 Printer Proof, Correspondence, 3 books, Manuscript Scan and Conversion, Typeset, Masters, Custom Cover, ISBN, Promo in Mink, 1 issue of Mink Magazine, Consultation, POD upload.

www.ingramcontent.com/pod-product-compliance
Lightning Source LLC
Chambersburg PA
CBHW052331220526
45472CB00001B/368